PREFACE

This book was written for the purpose of developing a BASS DRUM TECHNIQUE.

I hope that mastery of these exercises will help you have greater flexibility.

Colin Bailey

First Printing May 1964

To access audio visit:
www.halleonard.com/mylibrary
Enter Code
4842-6003-0273-5620

ISBN 978-0-7935-9159-6

HAL•LEONARD®
CORPORATION
7777 W. BLUEMOUND RD. P.O. BOX 13819 MILWAUKEE, WI 53213

Visit Hal Leonard Online at
www.halleonard.com

PLAYING THE EXERCISES

Two very important points are: where to place the foot on the footboard, and which part of the foot to use in order to get the best feel of the board. There is a "Sweet Spot" approximately $3\frac{1}{2}$" to 4" from the very top that gets the best leverage or "play" from the pedal. If you press this spot down with your finger, you will see that it gets better action than any other spot (higher or lower) on the board. The part of the foot I use is the very back of the toes, but the ball of the foot and the toe are acceptable also. The connection between the two is very important. Always try to keep your foot in the same spot on the board and use the same part of your foot. These things will make sure that you are consistant and accurate.

The technique I use on a single pedal is to bring the beater out of the Drum immediately after contact. This is achieved by using a lighter touch on the footboard, not pressing down hard, which automatically buries the beater into the head. Although you have to press down to feel the beats, it is not the main focal point of the technique. The volume required is decided by how far back you bring the beater, and the strength or velocity of the ankle stroke. I always keep the beater coming out of the Drum no matter how many beats are being played. Those are the three most important things, along with the sensible use of the footboard. I use a fairly slack spring tension because it gives the pedal more flexibility, especially when playing long or fast groups of beats.

I keep the heel down most of the time, only lifting when more speed is needed than I can play heel down. The lift I use is only $\frac{1}{4}$" to $\frac{1}{2}$" which is all the technique requires. The heel can be raised all the time as long as it's no higher than that, because lifting higher interferes with the mechanics of the technique. When I do lift, it's not until the beater strikes the head, and down again for Snare Drum beats or slower Bass Drum beats. The reason I do lift at all is to prevent tension in the front part of the leg. If you are using a double pedal, the heel can be lifted higher, but still concentrate on the "Sweet Spot" and the part of your foot. I recommend playing heel down until you have fairly good speed before trying my method, which is meant more for speed than very heavy playing. Of course, any technique can be applied in the use of this material.

ALTERNATE WAYS TO PLAY THE EXERCISES

Single Bass Drum beats, pages 5 and 6:

    1) Play down the entire page without stopping, one bar or the written two bars.

    2) Play eighth notes on Hi-Hat or Cymbal with the right hand. Play all top line with the left hand, and Bass Drum as written.

Double Bass Drum beats, pages 6, 7 and 8:

Play the first four exercises in succession (with no breaks). Other groups of these can be played in the same way. This applies to all categories in the book, and is good for continuity.

Sixteenth note patterns (1) on page 18, and (2) on page 19:

Play quarter or eighth notes on Hi-Hat, Cymbal, or Cymbal bell with the right hand. Play all top line with the left hand, and Bass Drum as written.

Contrapuntal Exercises, page 26 and 27:

Use quarter or eighth notes instead of written Cymbal pattern.

CONTROL DEVELOPMENT

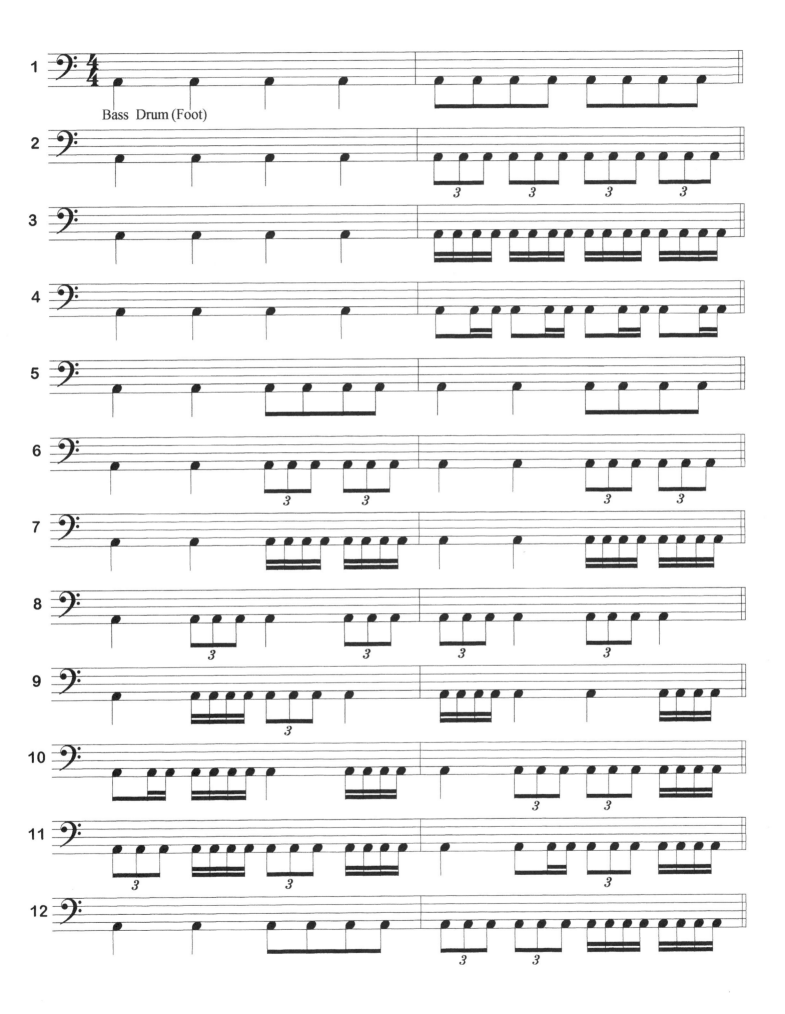

ACCENTS

SINGLE BASS DRUM BEATS
COMBINED WITH HANDS IN 16TH NOTE EXERCISES

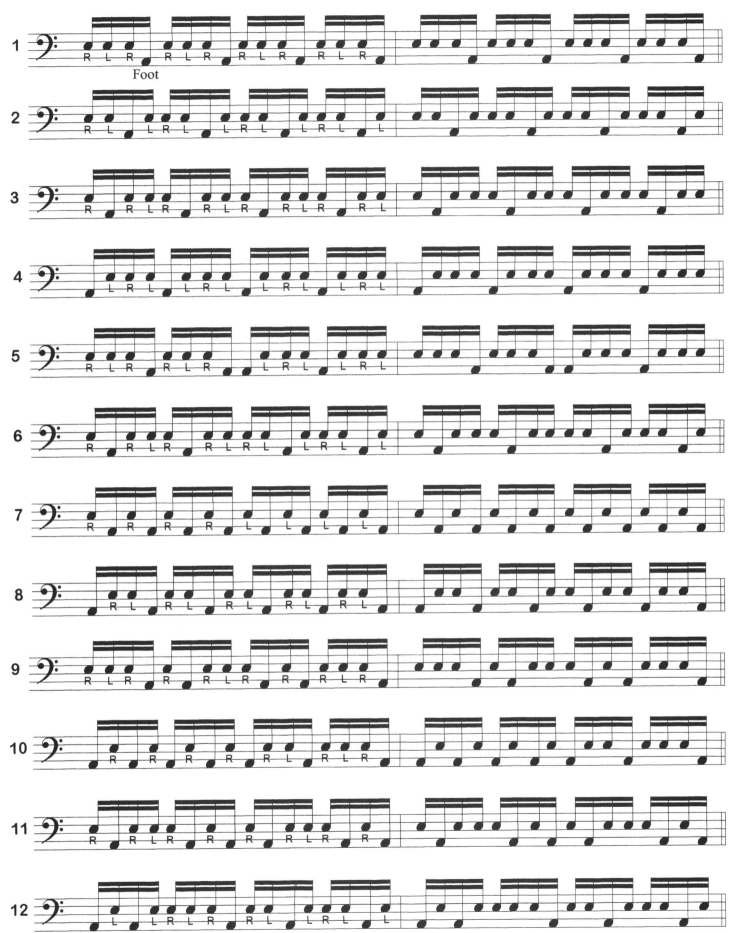

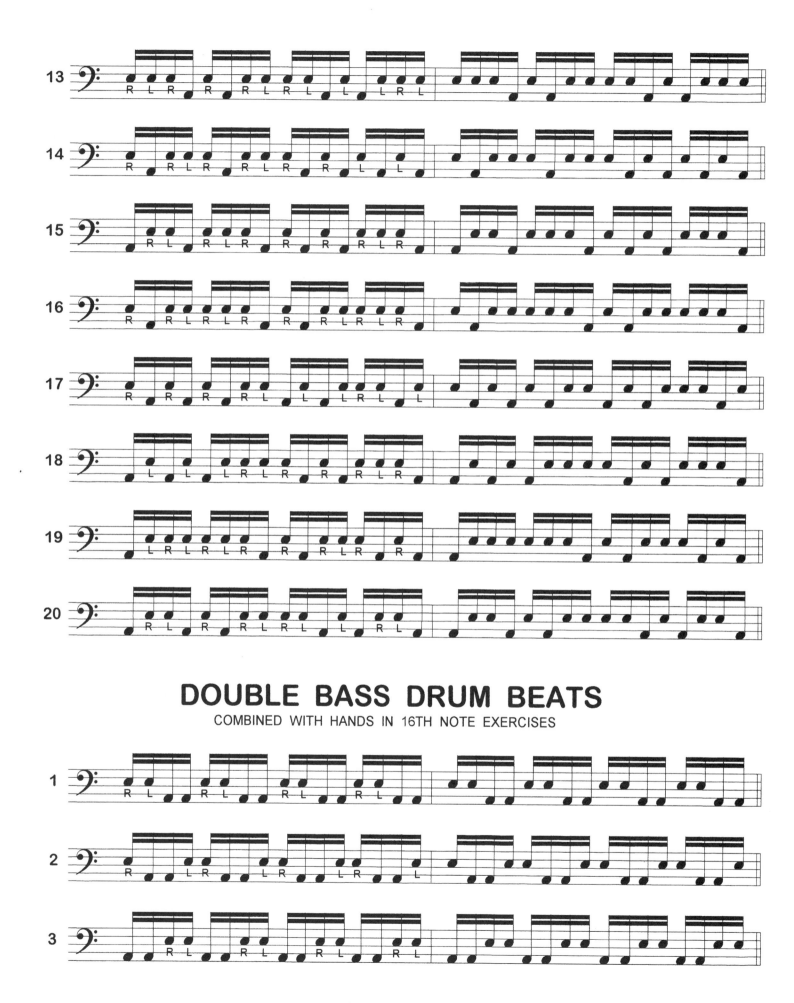

DOUBLE BASS DRUM BEATS
COMBINED WITH HANDS IN 16TH NOTE EXERCISES

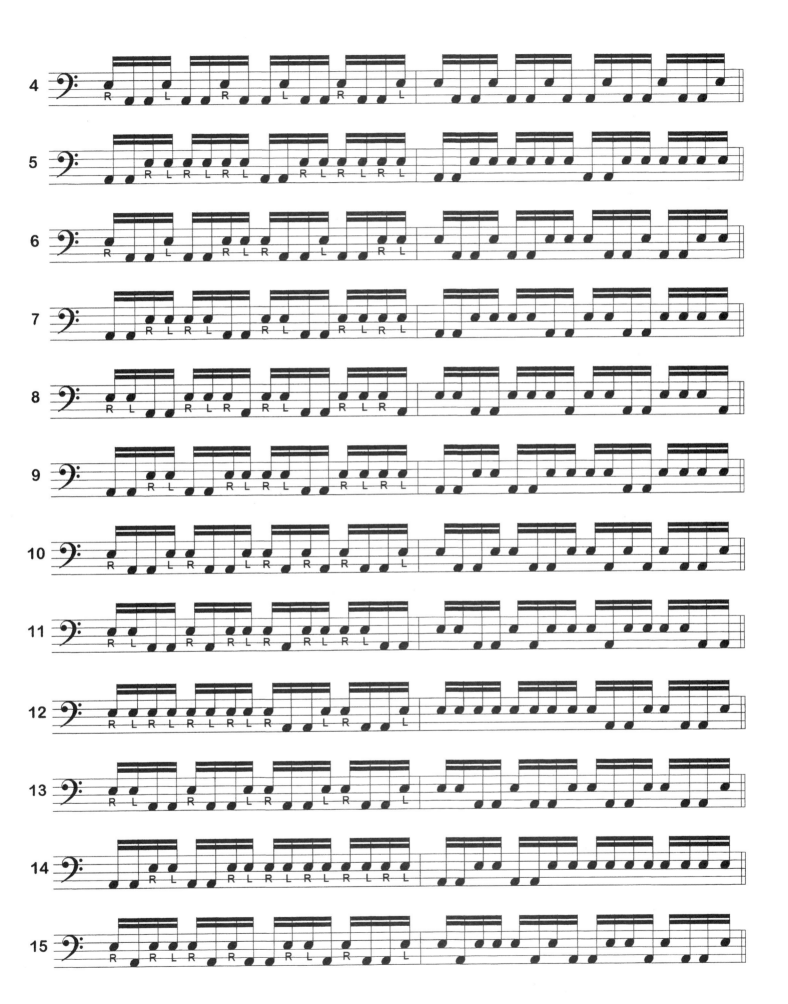

SINGLE AND DOUBLE

COMBINED WITH HANDS IN VARIATIONS OF PREVIOUS EXERCISES

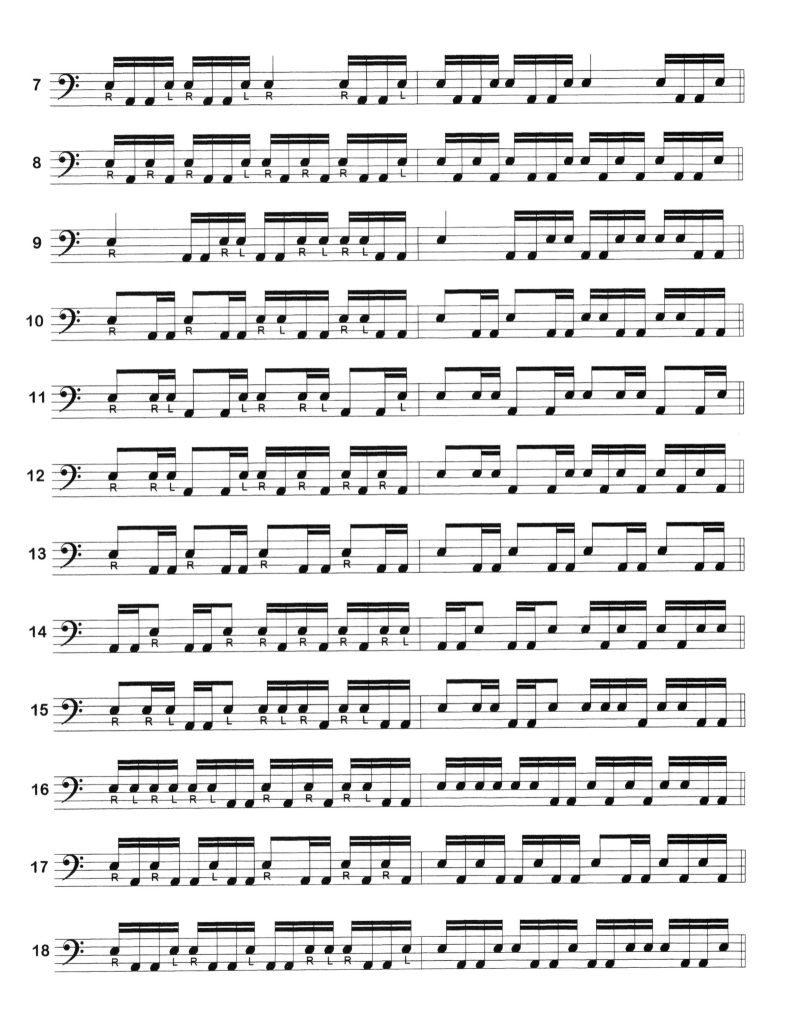

TRIPLE

BASS DRUM BEATS COMBINED WITH HANDS

VARIATIONS

USING 1 - 2 - 3 BASS DRUM BEATS COMBINED WITH HANDS

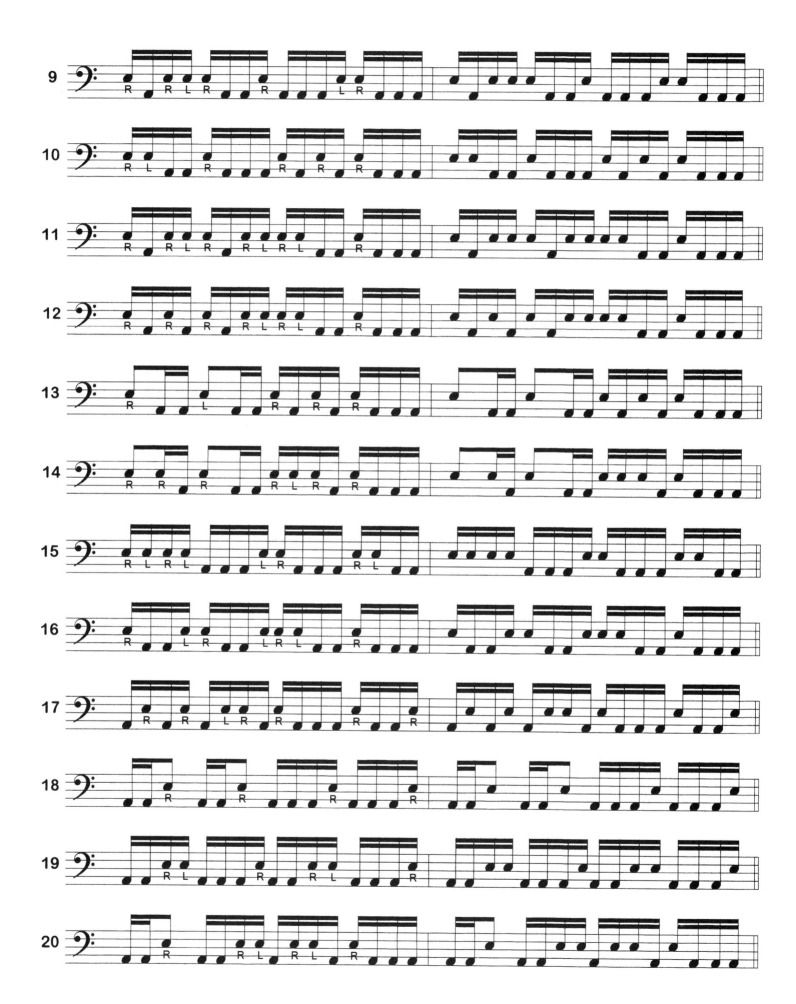

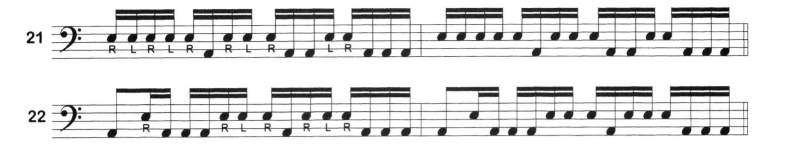

QUADRUPLE

BASS DRUM BEATS COMBINED WITH HANDS

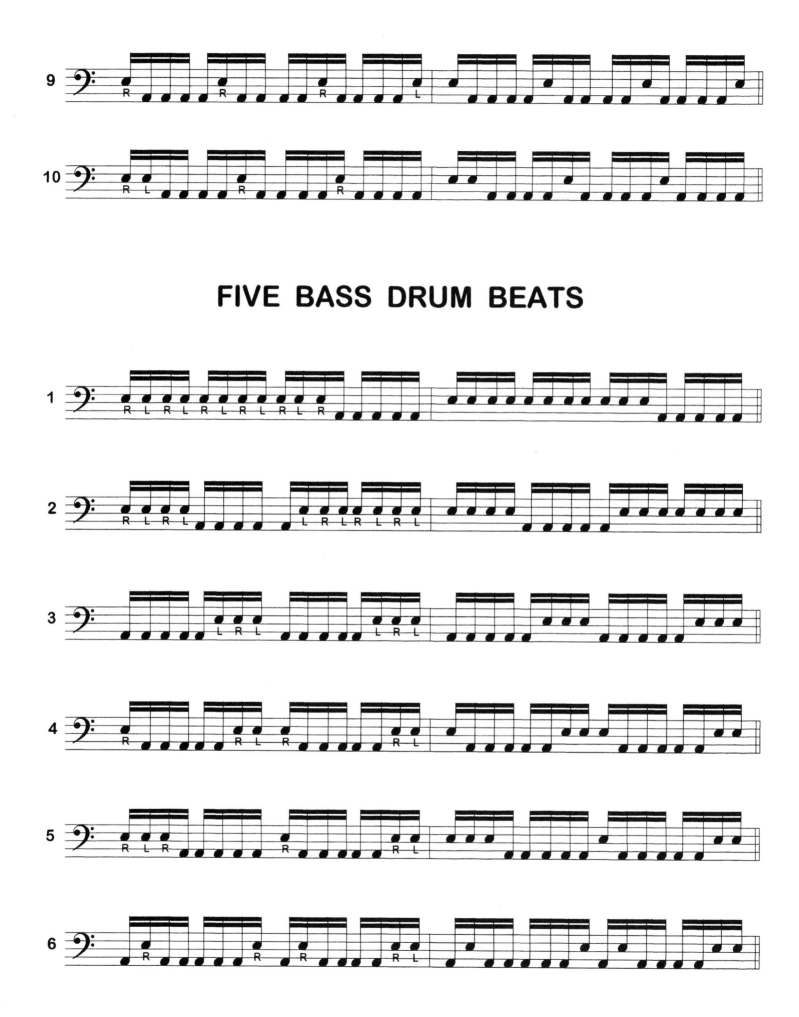

FIVE BASS DRUM BEATS

SIX BASS DRUM BEATS

SEVEN BASS DRUM BEATS

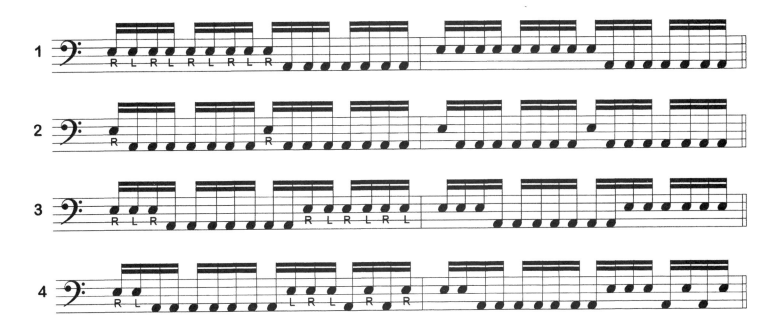

EIGHT BASS DRUM BEATS

ENDURANCE EXERCISE

FROM 4 TO 15 BASS DRUM BEATS

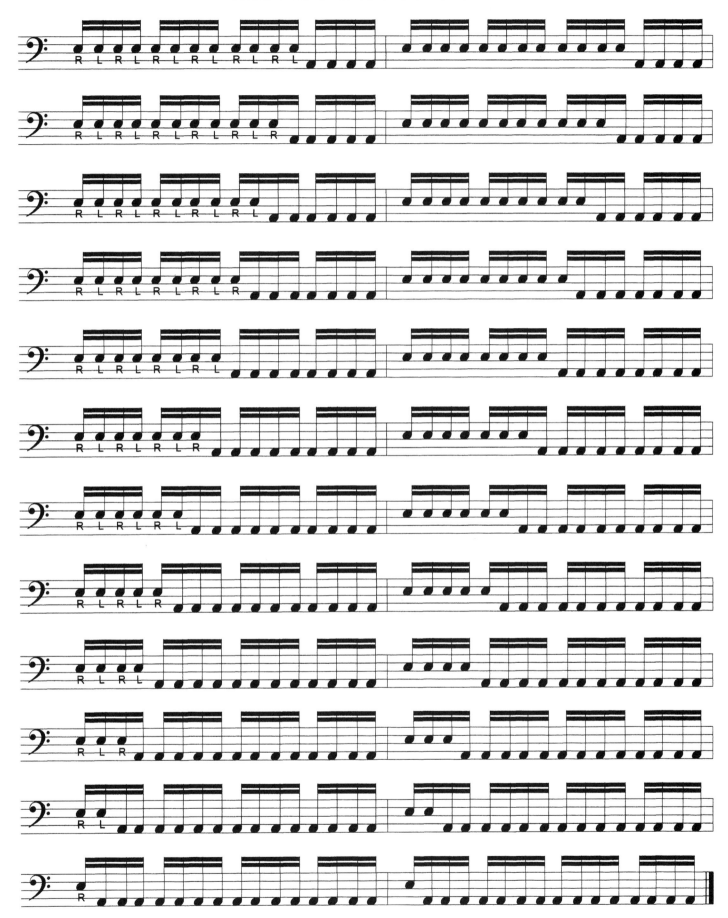

SIXTEENTH NOTE PATTERNS (1)

SIXTEENTH NOTE PATTERNS (2)

RUDIMENTAL EXERCISES

EMPLOYING THE USE OF THE BASS DRUM - ALTERNATE SNARE DRUM STICKING

SINGLE PARADDIDLE

DOUBLE PARADDIDLE

TRIPLE PARADDIDLE

FOUR STROKE RUFF

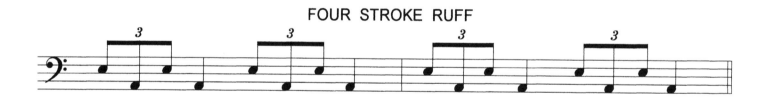

FIVE STROKE RUFF

SINGLE FLAM PARADDIDLE

DOUBLE FLAM PARADDIDLE

TRIPLE FLAM PARADDIDLE

SINGLE DRAG PARADDIDLE

DOUBLE DRAG PARADDIDLE

TRIPLE DRAG PARADDIDLE

THE LONG ROLL

22

COMBINATION TRIPLETS

FOUR BAR EXERCISES

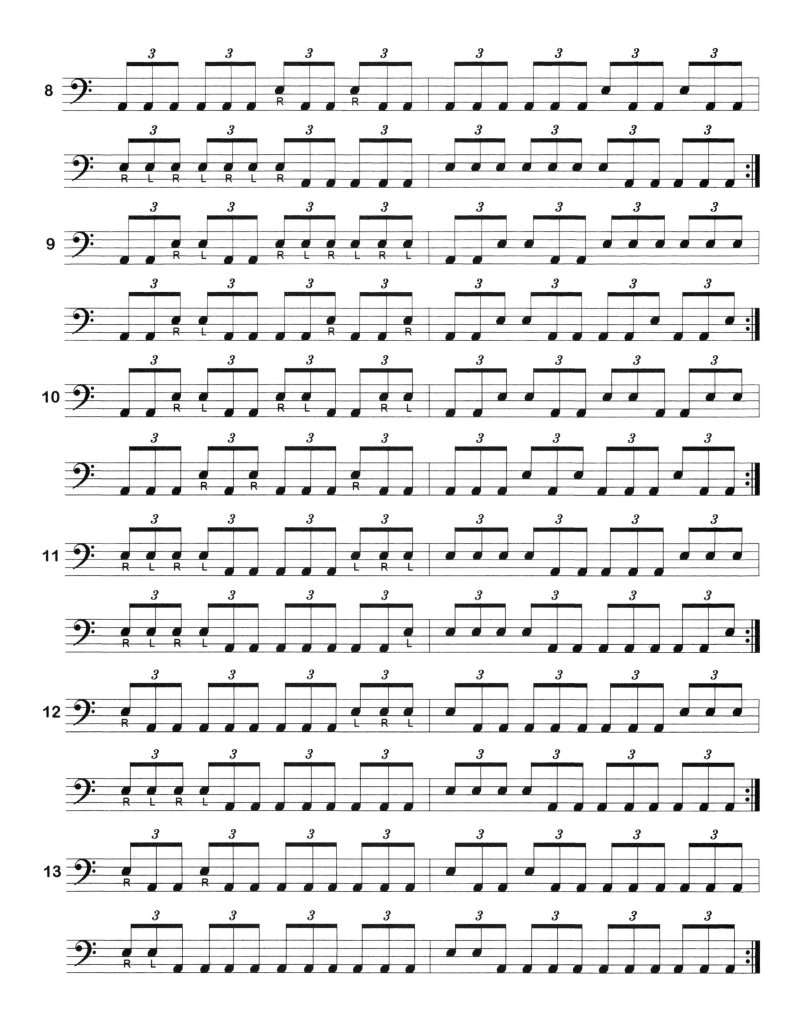

TWO BAR EXERCISES

CONTRAPUNTAL EXERCISES

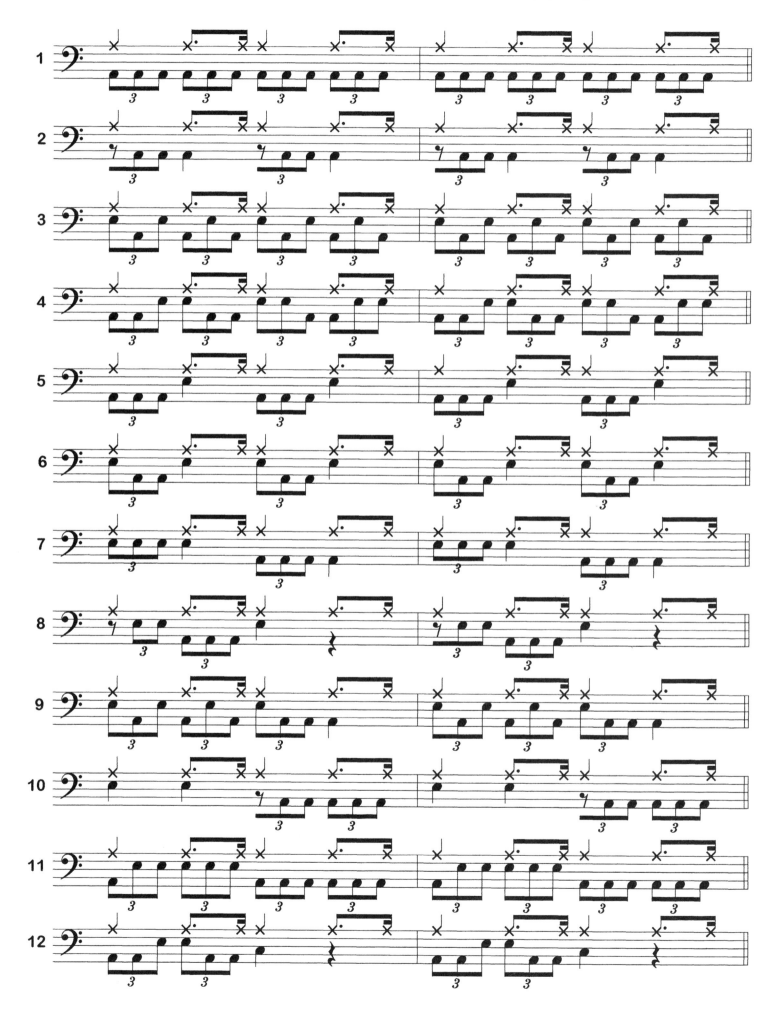

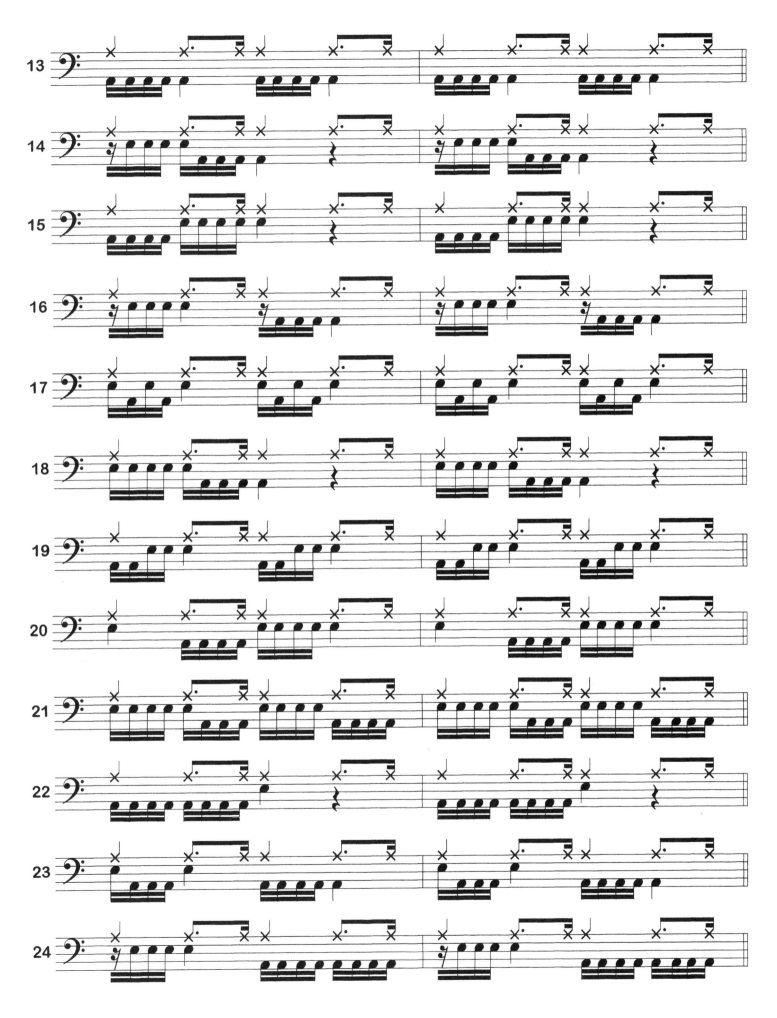

16th NOTE EXERCISES WITH TOM - TOMS

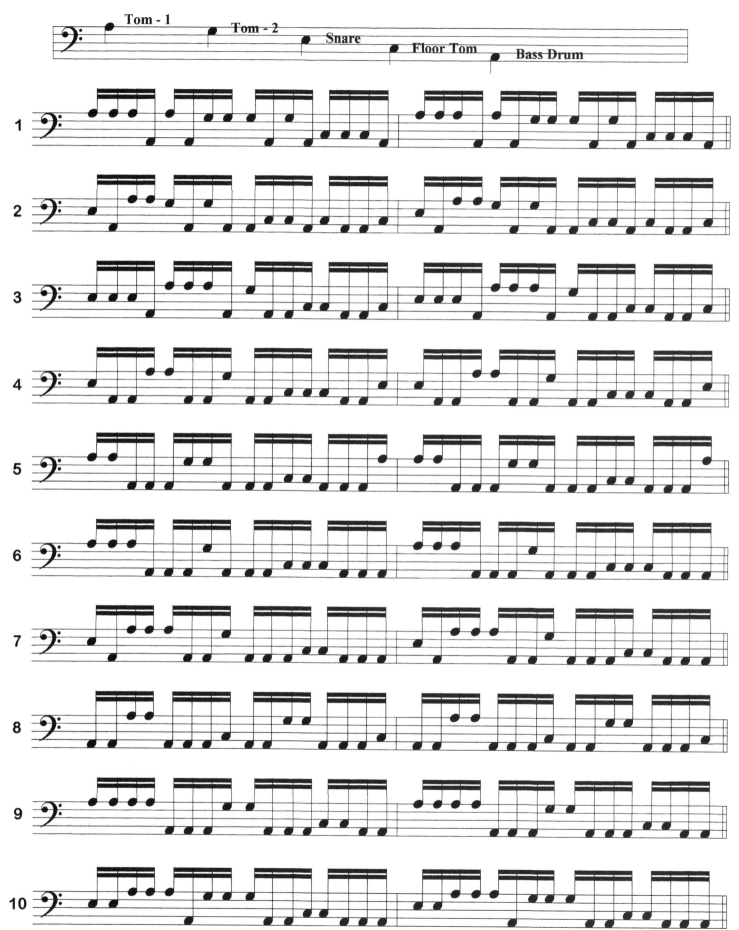

FOUR BAR SOLOS (FUNK STYLE)

TRIPLET SOLO

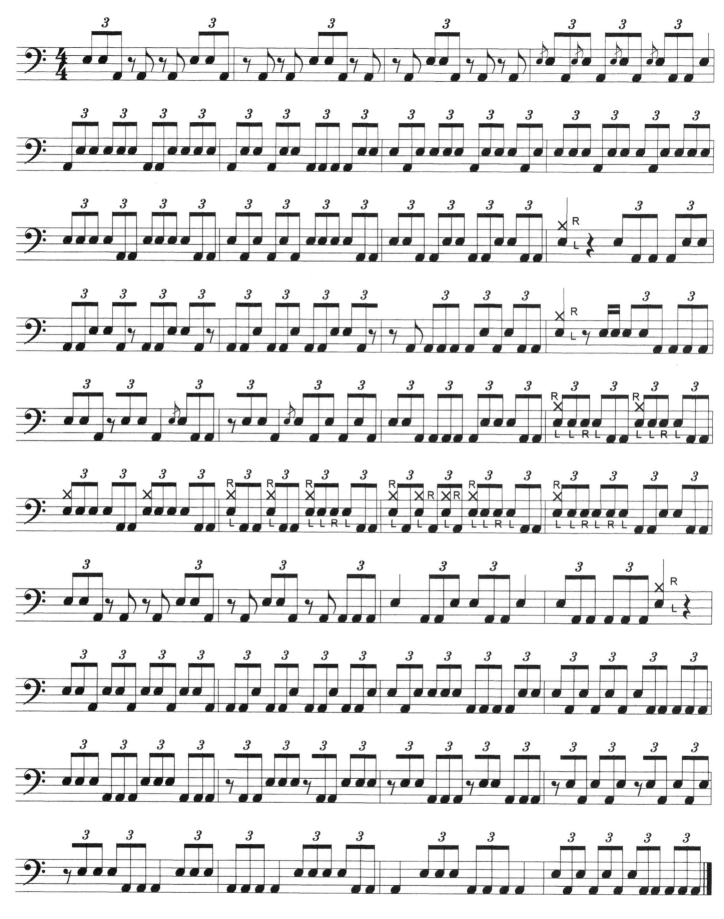

Concord Records C C D 4038 Victor Feldman Trio , " The Artful Dodger "

SOLO ON " AGITATION "

Agitation - Page 2